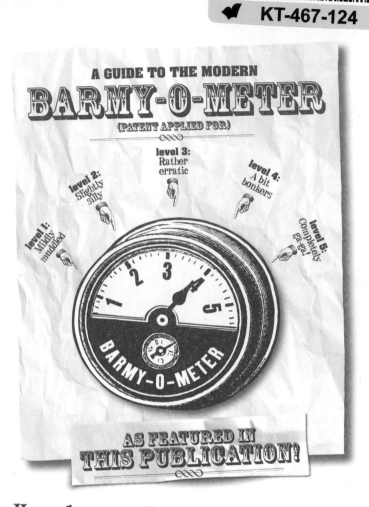

A GUIDE TO THE MODERN
BARMY-O-METER
(PATENT APPLIED FOR)

level 3: Rather erratic

level 2: Slightly silly

level 4: A bit bonkers

level 1: Mildly muddled

level 5: Completely ga-ga!

1 2 3 4 5

BARMY-O-METER

AS FEATURED IN
THIS PUBLICATION!

How do our Dictators, Rulers
and other Loony Leaders
rate on the Barmy-O-Meter?

Read on to find out!

THE WORLD'S WEIRDEST DICTATORS AND RULERS REVEALED

Leaders – they're supposed to be the best aren't they? Whether they're in charge of an expedition or running a country, leaders are meant to do a good job. Well that's not what this book is about; this book is about the mad, crazy, eccentric leaders and what they got up to.

Many of these people are **dictators** – people who have complete control of a country. Oddly enough, many dictators have certain things in common. Check out the dictator checklist opposite:

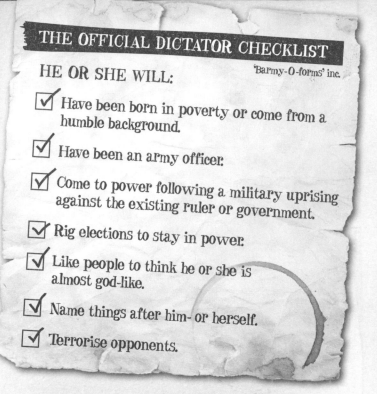

THE OFFICIAL DICTATOR CHECKLIST

'Barmy-O-forms' inc.

HE OR SHE WILL:

- ☑ Have been born in poverty or come from a humble background.
- ☑ Have been an army officer.
- ☑ Come to power following a military uprising against the existing ruler or government.
- ☑ Rig elections to stay in power.
- ☑ Like people to think he or she is almost god-like.
- ☑ Name things after him- or herself.
- ☑ Terrorise opponents.

Not everyone in this book is a dictator though. There are all types of leaders; from military generals who ignored their orders to explorers who couldn't read a map properly...

The thing that links them all is their behaviour – they all did something extraordinary, and that's why we remember them. Read on to find out about the daft things that leaders have said and done!

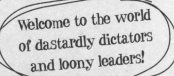

Welcome to the world of dastardly dictators and loony leaders!

The leader who whipped the sea

King Xerxes of Persia (519 –465 BC)

Water covers around three quarters of the world's surface, which can make getting from A to B quite inconvenient. This appears to have annoyed a number of rulers throughout history. For example, mad Roman emperor Caligula declared war on Poseidon, the Romans' god of the sea, and King Cnut of England tried to order the waves to turn back!

However, King Xerxes of Persia actually got so frustrated with the water that he had it punished. The reason he was so angry was that he and his army were on their way to Greece to expand his empire and the Aegean Sea was in the way. The narrowest point of the Aegean is between modern-day Turkey and Greece and is known as the Hellespont. Xerxes had a great plan to build a bridge across this kilometre-wide stretch of water.

Unfortunately the bridge wasn't strong enough and got washed away, so Xerxes did the obvious thing – he had the waves whipped 300 times as a punishment. He then built another bridge and invaded Greece – only to be defeated at the battle of Thermopylae.

The leader who banned beards

Enver Hoxha (1908–1985)

For some strange reason, dictators usually end up banning all sorts of different things. However, few dictators have been quite as random in what they banned as the Albanian leader Enver Hoxha. Can you guess which of the following Hoxha banned and which are made up?

The banned list:

- Beards
- Colour television
- Bananas
- Foreign journalists
- Religion
- Bright colours

And the correct answer is … ALL OF THEM!

Hoxha wasn't only mad about banning stuff – he was also paranoid about being invaded. As a result he built loads and loads of concrete defences along the country's border. In reality, as only one soldier could fit into each one they would have been pretty useless in the event of an invasion, but at least they kept the soldiers dry.

But I like my beard!

I name thee, me!

Saparmurat Niyazov (1940–2006)

BARMY RATING: 4 OUT OF 5

Both of Saparmurat Niyazov's parents died before his ninth birthday, so he grew up in an orphanage. By the age of 51, Niyazov had risen from these humble beginnings to become President of the state of Turkmenistan. And that's when things started to go a bit weird.

In true mad dictator style, Niyazov started to name things after himself. He started by naming the days of the week after himself and his family, and then the months too. Finally a meteorite was named after him.

Next came the mad building projects. Statues of the President started to appear around the country, and not just human-sized statues, but absolutely massive statues. Then there was the plan to build a man-made lake in the middle of the desert; and the plan for a new palace in the capital city – made entirely of ice!

As we have seen, dictators have a habit of banning stuff, too, and Niyazov doesn't let us down on that score either! He couldn't see the point of opera and ballet, so they were

banned. As was playing radios in
cars; playing music in public; young men
having long hair; and goatee beards.

Finally, to prove that the President knew best, his own book
was made required reading in every school. Unfortunately,
by the time of his death the country was wracked with
poverty – it seems the President didn't know best after all.

Niyazov meteorite

It's not fair, Janet!

Humph!

MAD, BAD

and truly sticky

ENDINGS

Fools!

Attila the Hun (406–453 AD)

From 434 to 453 AD a little-known people called the Huns rose up to become one of the most fearsome fighting forces central Europe had ever seen. At their head was a leader called Attila, who united the various Hun tribes and created an empire that stretched from Germany in the west to the Balkans in the East. The Huns were so frightening that even the Romans paid them to stay away.

And how did this mighty leader Attila die? Was it in a battle? Was he fighting against insurmountable odds?

No, he died from a nosebleed.

That's right; he had a nosebleed on his wedding night that turned out to be fatal! What a way to go!

CrackPot Quiz Question

Q. Lord Byron – the army officer, not the poet – fought for King Charles I during the English Civil War (1642–1651). During the Battle of Marston Moor, did Lord Byron ...?

a) Hide under a bush;

b) Ignore his orders and lose the battle for the King;

c) Do a daring solo raid that won the battle for the King.

And the answer ... b)!

Lord Byron (he was made a lord just before the battle) was clearly an impatient and easily bored man. He had orders to keep his troops on the right-hand-side of the King's army and – this is the important bit – STAY THERE.

Unfortunately Lord Byron got bored and decided to charge instead. His troops got bogged down in the marsh and were routed by the enemy, led by Oliver Cromwell (see pages 34–35). Worse still, the right-hand-side of the King's forces was left exposed and Cromwell's troops attacked from there and the King lost the battle!

11

Did They Really Do That?

DWIGHT D EISENHOWER (1890–1969)

'Any man who wants to be president is either an egomaniac* or crazy.'

Wise words indeed, but what does that make Mr Eisenhower who was President of the USA from 1953–1961?

Egomaniac or crazy? →

*An egomaniac is a person who is obsesessed with him or herself.

The leader who inspired Dracula

Vlad III (1431–1476)

Ha ha, this hat ain't blowing away!

Do you ever wonder where authors get their ideas from? Bram Stoker's most famous book is *Dracula* and he got the name of his vampire from a ruler of Wallachia (in present-day Romania) called Vlad Tepes – also known as Vlad Dracul.

Vlad didn't go round biting people and drinking their blood, but he did have a reputation for being cruel and blood-thirsty. His favourite form of punishment was stabbing people through with sharpened poles and leaving them on display when they died. This unfortunate habit earned him the nickname Vlad the Impaler.

The pointy sticks weren't the end of his cruelty. Once he was so annoyed when guests to his court didn't remove their hats that he had the hats stuck on to their heads.

'I shall attack using...

Hannibal (247 – 183 BC)

If you had to lead an animal across snow-covered mountains,
which would you choose? A mountain goat? Perfect.
An elephant? Um, perhaps not.

For many years Rome was at war with Carthage, a powerful
city in modern-day Tunisia. Carthage had a great military
leader, Hannibal, who had a
brilliant plan to invade Italy and
attack the Romans. He planned
to catch them by surprise with
his secret weapon –

elephants'

BARMY RATING: 4 OUT OF 5

war elephants! The only problem was he had to get them across a huge mountain range called the Alps.

You might think big animals like elephants would struggle up a mountain, but actually they're quite sure-footed – the biggest challenge was keeping them fed. Hannibal managed to get most of his 37 elephants and 50,000 troops safely across the mountains and launch a series of crushing attacks on the Romans, using his war elephants to devastating effect. The Romans had never been so badly beaten.

Unfortunately for Hannibal it wouldn't last. In 202 BC Hannibal was eventually defeated – and it was all because of those elephants. At the battle of Zama, the Romans deliberately made so much noise that the elephants got scared and started attacking Hannibal's soldiers instead! It was the beginning of the end for Hannibal and for Carthage. By 146 BC Hannibal was dead, Rome was victorious and Carthage was levelled to the ground.

Did They Really Do That?

Queen Tomyris (about 530 BC)

King Cyrus the Great of Persia ruled what was, at the time, the greatest empire that the world had ever seen. He was a great military leader and a clever politician, too. However, he made a mistake when he decided to take the lands of the Massagetae people of what is now in the area of Kazakhstan and Uzbekistan.

In around 530 BC, the Massagetae were ruled by the fearsome Queen Tomyris. She rejected Cyrus's proposal of marriage, and she was even less impressed when he invaded her territory. Imagine how cross she was when Cyrus tricked and captured her son – who then killed himself out of shame.

Gathering her troops she gave the Persian army a rather unexpected walloping. Cyrus himself was killed and legend has it that Tomyris cut off his head and used his skull as a drinking cup for the rest of her life.

That's one woman you didn't want to cross.

Ming the Merciless

Ming the Merciless was the inter-galactic super-villain from the Flash Gordon comics, radio and TV programmes, and films. He was emperor of the planet Mongo (not the coolest name in the galaxy, is it?) and he seemed to get his kicks from trying to take over the universe and by destroying planets.

Needless to say Ming always lost out to Flash Gordon, a human from Earth who ended up on Mongo with a couple of companions. You would think an intergalactic super-villain would have no problem defeating three normal humans, but he lost – time after time after time.

What was pretty cool though (apart from his name) was his Fu Manchu-style moustache (see page 79).

The leaders who wanted more statues

Ariki Mau

Ariki Mau is the name given to the tribal chiefs of Easter Island – the Pacific Ocean island famous for the large stone carvings of giant heads. Unfortunately, one theory suggests that these amazing sculptures proved to be Easter Island's downfall.

The Ariki Mau encouraged the islanders to keep building statues. But, this meant more and more trees had to be cut down to be used as rollers to move the statues to their final positions. Eventually there were no trees left.

This caused three major problems:

1 - The islanders couldn't build canoes, which meant they couldn't go fishing.

2 - No wood meant no building material for new houses, so people were forced to live in caves.

3 - The roots of the trees had stopped the soil from getting washed away. With the trees gone, the soil eroded, making growing crops very difficult.

As a result, the population of Easter Island declined rapidly – a stark warning to the world about cutting down too many trees!

MAD ABOUT...
THE GIRL

Sometimes boys do stupid things to impress girls and Mark Antony (83–30 BC), co-ruler of Rome, was no exception. He was so infatuated with Cleopatra, the female pharaoh of Egypt (see pages 52-53), that he made rather a foolish decision.

Mark Antony needed money to fight a war and Cleopatra had loads of it. Cleopatra needed an ally to keep her on the throne. And when the two met they fell in love and married – ahhhh. Mark Antony decided they would rule together!

But, there were two problems...

1 - Mark Antony was only co-ruler of Rome. One of the other rulers was called Octavian and he was not impressed with Antony's plan to shunt him out of the picture.

2 - Mark Antony was already married. To make matters worse, his old wife was Octavian's sister!

Awkward!

Civil war followed and Mark Antony lost both the war and his life.

Thomas Becket (1118–1170)

The Archbishop of Canterbury during the reign of King Henry II, Thomas Becket (also known as Thomas a Beck and Thomas a Becket) is famous for being murdered by three drunken knights. The story goes that the King was so fed up with Becket that he (reputedly) said 'Who will rid me of this turbulent priest?' The knights overheard the King and decided to show him. They rode to Canterbury Cathedral and killed Becket on 29th December 1170. Talk about a rubbish Christmas present.

What makes this all interesting is that King Henry and Becket had been great friends. Henry liked a good time and Becket knew how to have one. He had his own private zoo, for example, and kept a whole flock of parrots.

trained monkeys

But best of all he had a troop of monkeys! And not only that, he taught them how to ride horses.

When Becket went on an official visit to France he took his horseriding monkeys with him – much to the amazement of the French (and probably the English that they passed too). Now that's travelling in style!

BARMY RATING: 3 OUT OF 5

MAD, BAD

and truly sticky

ENDINGS

Fools!

Maximilien de Robespierre (1758–1794)

The French Revolution of 1789–1799 saw the overthrow of the French monarchy and control of the country placed in the hands of Parliament. One of the leading figures in the Revolution and of the government was Maximilien de Robespierre.

He was a brilliant and ruthless leader. He had political opponents executed for treason during a so-called 'Reign of Terror' which lasted for over a year.

The official method of execution was the guillotine – a machine that chopped off people's heads. More than 12,000 people died on the guillotine during the Terror and perhaps as many as 250,000 died in prison or in fighting.

The killing sickened people and when Robespierre started to insist that France adopt a new religion of the Supreme Being, people got sick of him too. Robespierre was executed on the guillotine in 1794.

Did They Really Do That?

GENERAL FERDINAND FOCH (1851–1929)

'My centre is giving way, my right is in retreat; situation excellent. I shall attack.'

This, apparently, was the crazy message that French General Foch sent to a fellow officer during World War I as the battle raged around Marne in northern France. Despite the fact that his forces were crumbling around him, his counter-attack had some effect – actually forcing the German army to retreat.

Foch's actions got him promoted. Unfortunately the soldiers under his command paid the price for these daring counter-attacks – most of them didn't survive.

World War wonder

Lieutenant Colonel 'Mad Jack' Churchill (1906–1996)

When you think of World War II and its weapons it's probably stuff like tanks, Spitfires and the first nuclear bombs. But this wasn't the kind of equipment that British Army Commando leader John Churchill was interested in. No, his preferred weapons were a longbow and a sword.

These weapons were really old-fashioned but they still proved to be useful. On one night-time raid with one other soldier, Churchill, armed only with his sword, managed to capture 41 German soldiers. He was also the last person to kill an enemy soldier with a bow and arrow.

His old-fashioned choice of weaponry wasn't the only thing that set Lieutenant Colonel Churchill apart. He was also fond of playing the bagpipes. He used to practise whenever the mood took him, which could be at any time of day or night – much to the annoyance of his fellow soldiers.

That even included when going into battle. Apparently the soldiers in his regiment would follow Churchill anywhere – but maybe they secretly hoped the bagpipes might get shot!

Churchill's strange behaviour continued after the war. The River Severn has a tidal bore, a large wave that travels upstream each year at the spring high tide. Churchill was the first person to surf this wave – and he did it on a board he designed and built himself.

MADE-UP MANIACS

Emperor Palpatine/ Darth Sidious

Emperor Palpatine is from the *Star Wars* films and is the public face of the power-hungry, treacherous politician who rises to power in the new Empire. Now, that's bad enough, but he has an even more evil side – Darth Sidious.

This unpleasant character is a Sith Lord, an expert in the dark side of the Force (the power that binds the Universe together). By the end of the *Star Wars* films the character appears in his Darth Sidious guise all the time – proving that a thirst for total power not only corrupts but also makes you very wrinkly.

EMPEROR TAMERLANE (1336–1405)

Terrible Towers

When Persian emperor Tamerlane (1336–1405), also known as Timur the Lame thanks to his limp, was building his huge empire he knew how to get ahead. After defeating an army he would leave behind huge towers of skulls as a warning to his enemies.

Animals didn't fare much better with the maniacal warlord. The Indian city of Delhi was defended by the Indians' war elephants. Tamerlane heard that elephants were scared of flames, so he set fire to his own camels and charged them at the elephants. True enough the elephants panicked and ran away and Tamerlane took the city. Bet the camels got the hump, though.

Who's in charge?

Jean-Bédel Bokassa (1921–1996)

In 1965, Jean-Bédel Bokassa, a colonel in the army of the Central African Republic, led a military coup, or uprising, that overthrew the country's leadership. He promptly proclaimed himself to be the country's President, Prime Minister, Commander-in-Chief of the armed forces and leader of the Central African Republic's one political party – that way everyone knew who was in charge.

Bokassa then went on a spending spree. He set up a large private hunting estate, built a private airstrip nearby and bought a private jet liner to go on it. He even had a uniform made that had to be strengthened to carry the weight of all the medals he awarded himself.

By 1976, Bokassa had decided that being President was a little bit *ordinary*, so had himself crowned. The coronation cost an absolute fortune and left the country deeply out of pocket.

Fools!

MAD, BAD
and truly sticky
ENDINGS

Draco (about 650–600 BC)

Draco was responsible for writing down the laws of the Athenians in ancient Greece – and he achieved a well-deserved reputation for being really, really harsh. His list of punishments was as long as it was cruel. You could be put to death for stealing a cabbage, or sent into slavery for being in debt. Despite this people seemed to like him – perhaps they were too scared to say otherwise!

In those days throwing your cloak at someone was a sign of appreciation. When Draco made a public appearance, people began throwing their cloaks. And then the people behind them threw theirs. And then more and more people threw cloaks. There was a lot of appreciating going on that day. Too much appreciating!

The pile of cloaks grew higher and higher. Draco disappeared from view. And still the cloaks rained down. Underneath the pile Draco was trapped – and apparently died of overheating!

The lady who go

Boudicca (c.61 AD)

Sometimes people do things without thinking of what the consequences might be. That was certainly true of the Romans in 61 AD (or possibly 60 AD, no one is quite sure) when they challenged a woman called Boudicca. Her husband had been head of the Iceni tribe (who lived in what is now East Anglia), and when he died he left his lands to be shared by his two daughters and the new Roman emperor, Nero. However, the Romans decided to take all the Iceni land for themselves. To make matters worse, they then assaulted Boudicca and her two daughters.

This made Boudicca angry – as you might expect. In fact she was very, very angry; so angry she started a revolt. She had a lot of support from the Iceni tribe who were fed up with Roman rule. She led her army to destroy the cities of Colchester, London and what is now St Albans, murdering everyone she could find. She and her army were finally defeated in a great battle against Roman forces.

Ultimately she may have lost, but the Romans learnt a lesson about being careful who you annoy.

her own back

MAD ABOUT...
MEN'S CLOTHES

Anne Bonny (1702–1782) and fellow female pirate Mary Read (1685–1721) were two seafaring ladies. However, since no women were allowed aboard ships at the time they had to be rather clever about it. In order to be pirates they had to dress in men's clothes. To make sure their deception was complete, they acted just as ferociously as their crew mates. When the crew finally realised they were women, the girls had already proved themselves to be at least the equal of any male pirate!

I say, these trousers are comfortable.

Yes, I don't miss skirts at all!

Nice city – what shall we call it?

Alexander the Great (356 – 323 BC)

Alexander the Great became leader of the Macedonians at the age of 20. Over the next 13 years he would create the biggest empire the world had ever seen. It stretched from Macedonia, in southern Europe, to Pakistan, and covered in the region of five million square kilometres (two million square miles).

He inspired a near fanatical loyalty from his army and proved to be a talented ruler, blending the best of the ancient Greek culture that he grew up with, with the local traditions and customs of those countries he invaded. He even wore local costumes. Was there anything he couldn't do?

Well yes there was actually – he was pretty rubbish at naming cities. Alexander is said to have founded up to 70 cities and he named 20 of them after himself. Not much imagination there. Cities called Alexandria popped up all over the place like a rash. One time he did name a city Bucephela – but this was named after his favourite horse, which had just died. And guess what the full name of the city was:

Alexandria Bucephela!

Like father ...

Oliver and Richard Cromwell (1599–1658 and 1626–1712)

By 1642, the English Parliament had begun to get thoroughly fed up with their King, Charles I. He didn't treat them with any respect, did his best to ignore them and generally acted like he was God's gift to England – mainly because he believed God had decided he should be in charge.

Parliament, led by Oliver Cromwell, decided enough was enough and civil war broke out. On one side were the King and his supporters and on the other side were Cromwell and his supporters. They believed that Parliament should run the country and not some daft king. The Civil War lasted for nine years and Cromwell's forces won. In 1649, Charles I was executed and England became a republic – hurray! Let's have a party to celebrate!

Oh no you won't! You see Cromwell turned out to be even more crazy than the King. He was a Puritan, a member of a religion that didn't believe in fuss and show. This was great for quiet praying, but pretty rubbish for having fun. Suddenly things that ordinary people quite enjoyed started to get banned.

like son...

It was quite a long list and included make up, theatre, and even Christmas!

For the poor people of England it felt like fun had been forbidden!

And things got even worse when Oliver Cromwell died and his son, Richard, took over. Now, Oliver had banned lots of things and had gone to war in Ireland, but at least he was a good organiser and had set the foundation for the Parliament we know today. Richard, on the other hand, had his father's lack of humour combined with none of his talents. He was a disaster and people began to wonder why he was in charge. Surely a son taking over when his father died was just like when the royals were heading up the country?

In 1660, people decided enough was enough. The royal family was invited back and Charles II became King. And this time people were allowed to have a party!

Keep it down!

Hurray for cabbage!

Captain James Cook (1728–1779)

When Captain James Cook of *HMS Endeavour* started feeding his crew cabbage, lemon juice and malt, it's fair to say that he wasn't going to win many friends – or good restaurant reviews. He was saving their lives though!

Exploring the high seas aboard a sailing ship was a dangerous game. Storms, huge waves and rocks could all put a sailor's life in peril, but one of the biggest killers was actually not getting their five a day!

That's right, not getting enough vitamins – especially vitamin C – often led to a particularly nasty disease called scurvy. Sailors with scurvy would notice their skin going black, then their teeth would fall out, breathing would become difficult, their arms would be stiff, their gums would swell, their hearing and eyesight would be affected and their breath would smell. Scurvy this bad was usually fatal.

Captain Cook was famous for discovering Australia, which probably came as a surprise to the Aborigines who already lived there. However, his explorations were hugely important and he couldn't have done it with a dead crew. Cook realised that there was a link between vitamins and scurvy so he fed his crew sauerkraut (a cabbage dish) and lemon syrup. For the most part it worked and changed the diet of sailors forever!

So think about that next time you turn your nose up at broccoli!

Some more cabbage, Jenkins?

Oh yes please, Captain, I feel fit as a fiddle!

MAD ABOUT...
PANTS

The Crusades were a series of wars fought between Christians and Muslims from 1095 to 1272. Most of the fighting took place in the Middle East and around the city of Jerusalem (in modern-day Israel).

The Christian soldiers were known as crusaders; and one of the craziest crusaders of all was Godfrey of Bouillon. This French knight was in charge of the crusaders trying to take control of Jerusalem from the Muslims in 1099. The battle was long, hard and bloody; and the crusaders won. And how did Godfrey celebrate?

By walking around the streets in his pants! Perhaps he didn't want to get blood on his clothes.

GEORGE W BUSH (1946–)

'I know the human being and fish can co-exist peacefully.'

When campaigning in the year 2000, Bush said he had no plans to pull down a dam to help fish get upriver. Then he went a little off-script. We'd love to tell you why he said it (he was president of the USA at the time) or what he was talking about; but we can't. Perhaps he was worried about a major fish revenge attack?

Let's be friends!

Sure!

The extraordinary life of Mr Train

George Train (1829–1904)

George Train is possibly the most remarkable man you've never heard of. There is a famous book called *Around the World in 80 Days* and it's about a man who bets he can travel around the globe in, well 80 days like the title says (this was in the days before aeroplanes). Well that author got the idea from George Train because he had attempted to do just that – and had succeeded against all the odds!

It would be a bigger adventure than most people would ever have in their lives, but that was only part of the amazing story of George Train...

THE LIFE & TIMES

END OF THE LINE FOR TRAIN

George Train, explorer, adventurer, politician and genuine eccentric, passed away today aged 74.

Perhaps inspired by his own name, George Train travelled the world building tramways and railways in various countries. His travels led him into some surprising situations. For example, he was asked to be the leader of Australia. He refused, but did run for the presidency of the USA. He failed at that, but then tried to see if people were interested in him being dictator of the USA. People weren't, so George busied himself with whatever was fashionable or interesting at the time – even turning vegetarian.

A colourful character, Train had his brushes with the law. He was accused of murder and of embezzlement (stealing money by deception). But was found innocent on both occasions.

Ever the eccentric, George would only ever shake hands with himself and spent the last years of his life sitting on a park bench talking to the pigeons. His like will never be seen again.

BARMY RATING: 2 OUT OF 5

The leader who didn't like painting

Aurangzeb (1618–1707)

Do you like music? Or painting? Or finding out fun stuff from the past? Then the last place you would want to be was India during the reign of the Mughal emperor Aurangzeb. The mad Mughal didn't like any of the above and had them all banned – even writing about old stuff. Why? Perhaps he didn't like his history lessons.

It's a shame as he would have really missed out. Imagine there being no music or art – or books like this one!

Sadly children, this will be our last piano lesson for a while...

Cool!

The emperor who wasn't paying attention

Sun Hao (242–284 AD)

Often dictators get rid of all their opponents because they fear being overthrown themselves. Much of their time in power is spent looking out for trouble. The case of Chinese emperor Sun Hao is a good example of what can happen if you aren't really paying attention.

In the 200s, China was divided into three different kingdoms. Sun Hao was the head of the Wu dynasty, which controlled the south-eastern part of the country. Much was expected of the promising young emperor – but he delivered very little. He proved to be pretty useless at controlling his lands. He had opponents tortured and killed – and by opponents we mean anyone he didn't like. He was also very superstitious and worried about bad omens.

As Sun Hao was spending all his time with cruelty and lucky charms, he wasn't prepared when his empire was invaded by the Jin dynasty next door. Sun Hao was captured and his lands taken over by the Jin.

Joseph Stalin
(1878–1953)

When Russian leader Vladimir Lenin died in 1924, his successor, Joseph Stalin decided a memorial should be built. As Lenin had been a huge figure in Russian history, the monument needed to be impressive.

He decided that a statue should be built of Lenin; and – to show the world how great Russia was – it was going to be absolutely ginormous, the biggest structure on the planet!

Work started on the mammoth project in 1937. The foundations alone took two years to build but then World War II happened and the project was abandoned, never to be taken up again.

The commander who attacked her own fleet

Artemisia I of Caria (about 480 BC)

Being a successful woman in a world dominated by men is tough – so it helps if you can be clever, talented and totally ruthless. Take Queen Artemisia of Caria for example.

When the Persian emperor Xerxes was invading Greece, Artemisia was his only female commander. Xerxes wanted to attack the Greek navy at Salamis. Artemisia advised him not to. He ignored her. Big mistake.

As Xerxes watched, the Persian navy suffered a terrible defeat. Artemisia was commanding one of the boats, but when it looked like she was in danger from a Greek ship, she promptly turned her boat round and rammed a Persian one. The Greeks, thinking she was one of theirs, left her alone. Xerxes, who thought she had attacked a Greek ship, praised her for her bravery.

Playing with FIRE

Guy Fawkes (1570–1606)

People have always been keen to complain about politicians and the government, but Guy Fawkes went further than most – he tried to blow them up!

Guy wasn't working alone; he was part of a group of 12 conspirators. They were all Catholics and the King, James I, was a Protestant. Their aim was to get rid of the King and replace him with someone else.

The plan was to fill a room in the cellars below Parliament with explosives and blow the whole lot up when the King arrived. The plan became known as the Gunpowder Plot!

Guy was the explosives expert and he was the man who was going to light the fuse. It was a risky operation.

On 4th November, Guy was discovered with the gunpowder, but the guards didn't arrest him. However, the next day the guards came back and Guy was arrested, tortured and executed. Strange? We think so!

Some historians think Guy and his guys were set up. The group of Catholics were able to rent rooms under Parliament; they were able to get their hands on lots of gunpowder - when all gunpowder was controlled by the government - and put it all under Parliament with no one noticing. Also, Guy wasn't arrested on the 4th even though he was standing next to the explosives. These historians argue that the arrests were made on the 5th because that was when the most publicity could be gained – just before Guy could set off the country's biggest firework display!

MAD, BAD
and truly sticky
ENDINGS

Fools!

Pope Urban IV (1318–1389)

The Pope is the leader of the Catholic Church, the largest of all the Christian religions. You would think that a religious leader would believe in peace and goodwill to all people – but Pope Urban IV certainly didn't!

As soon as he was elected as Pope he started to annoy his cardinals (senior members of the Catholic Church) with his arrogant, argumentative and insulting nature.

Urban liked a good war, too, and raised an army to attack the city of Naples, putting his nephew in charge.

The story goes that Urban died from his injuries after falling off a mule – but some people say he was probably poisoned. A sticky end either way.

Crackpot Quiz Question

Q. General Custer was defeated at the Battle of the Little Big Horn (1876) by Native American Indians. Was it because... ?

a) His troops were massively outnumbered;

b) He ignored orders and attacked a Native American camp without reinforcements;

c) He decided not to bring Gatling guns (an early type of machine gun) with him as they would slow him down.

And the answer is: All of the above! General Custer was a successful military leader during the American Civil War. Later, during the war with the Native American Indians, Custer discovered a large Indian camp and attacked it – without waiting for orders or reinforcements. The rest – and Custer – is history. He and all 209 of his troops died.

The dictator with wardrobe worries

Mobutu Sese Seko (1930–1997)

You might think that fashion is not a priority for dictators – having a country to run and all that – but not in the case of Mobutu Sese Seko. Mobutu came to power in the African country of Zaire (now the Democratic Republic of Congo) during a military takeover in 1965.

Once in power, Mobutu banned anything that looked too Western. Christian names were banned, for example, and even some styles of clothing got the thumbs down. Business suits were out and a new collarless suit he designed was in. Ties were banned and a new cravat-style neckerchief was made compulsory for office workers. Mobutu liked to accessorise his new-style suit with a type of hat called a toque, which he had made in leopard skin.

Mobutu also went on shopping trips abroad and visited Disneyland – all paid for by the coutry.

After 31 years of rule, the country was broke, and Mobutu had kept the country's wealth for himself. Eventually, he was overthrown and sent to live in exile (forbidden to live in his own country).

Crackpot Quiz Question

Q: What did Murad IV (1612–1640) ban during his reign over Turkey? Was it ...?

a) Smoking;

b) Coffee;

c) Chocolate.

It's a) and b)! Murad passed a law to say that anyone caught smoking a pipe would be put to death! And then he banned coffee too! What's more, Murad loved smoking pipes and drinking coffee with his friends.

Cleopatra (c.69–30 BC)

BARMY RATING: 3 OUT OF 5

It is a truth universally acknowledged that a queen in possession of a large fortune and worried about threats to her rule must be in need of a powerful ally – and that is exactly the position Cleopatra found herself in.

She was a pharaoh of ancient Egypt and needed help – and that help came in the regal shape of Julius Caesar, emperor of the Roman Empire. Unfortunately for both of them, Julius got stabbed in the back by his friends – literally – and was no more.

Happily though, Mark Antony – new co-ruler of Rome – appeared (see page 19). Attracted by Cleopatra's immense wealth and charismatic personality, he suggested they form a new alliance, which suddenly went pear-shaped when civil war broke out and Cleo and Mark found themselves on the losing side. Cleopatra was captured, but rather than suffer the humiliation of being made prisoner she had a poisonous snake called an asp smuggled into her room. She let the snake bite her and the rest (and she) was history.

an alliance...

MADE-UP MANIACS

Lord Voldemort

The evil wizard of the *Harry Potter* books and films is one of the top baddies of all time. He's so scary that people don't even want to say his name, instead calling him *'You know who'*. Crazy for power, he lets nobody get in the way of his plans; he bumps people off all the time and is said to like killing Muggles (non-magical humans) just for the fun of it.

As a child (called Tom Riddle) he is a handsome boy but as he gets older, and more evil, he becomes distorted and ugly. By the time the reader meets him he is truly terrifying with a skull-like head, red eyes and slitted nostrils.

Of course Voldemort loses in the end, proving crime (magical or not) doesn't pay.

The queen who wanted a simpler life

Marie Antoinette (1755–1793)

You might think being a queen is great. You get to boss people around and everyone does everything for you. However, Marie Antoinette, wife of King Louis XVI of France, begged to differ. She hated the stuffiness of being at the royal court and longed for a simpler life. Fortunately she was Queen so she was mega-rich. She spent around £4 million on building a fake tumble-down village complete with a working farm. Some stories claim she even dressed as a shepherdess and played with the sheep; though many historians are not sure this is true.

Either way, Marie spent a fortune building a pretty, fake village while real French peasants were starving to death. Not long after, there was a revolution in France and Marie Antoinette was executed.

Oh look at those pretty sheep, how divine!

CrackPot Quiz Question

Q. Can you guess the preferred pastime of top American gangster Al Capone? Was it ...?

a) Flower arranging;

b) Horse riding;

c) Writing love songs.

It's c)! He wrote love songs. Yep, mad, bad, let's-murder-all-our-enemies Al Capone wrote love songs. He even wrote one called Madonna Mia to his wife when he was in jail. We're not sure how much she liked it though – Capone ended up giving it to a priest instead.

The world's worst estate agent

Erik the Red (950—1003)

If you lived in a snowy country and you heard of a new country called Greenland, you might be quite interested in going to live there; especially if your own country was called Iceland. Greenland would probably sound nice and warm – all pleasant and, erm, green. This was exactly what the Viking Erik the Red was hoping people would think and managed to convince 500 people to move from Iceland to a new colony he set up up in a place he had just discovered – Greenland.

One problem – Greenland is an icy place battered by winds and sees daylight for only a couple of hours a day during the winter.

Cor blimey, this is a bit chilly!

Perhaps we shouldn't be so surprised that Erik stretched the truth a bit – after all, he found Greenland when he was exiled from Iceland for killing two people. So he was both a murderer and a teller of massive porkies.

57

LUCKY NUMBER NINE

Ne Win (1911–2002)

When Ne Win took charge of Burma (modern-day Myanmar) it was a relatively prosperous country. By the time he stepped down as leader in 1998, Myanmar was one of the poorest. So how did this happen?

Well much of it was due to Ne Win's bizarre decisions and behaviours, many of which were based on his lucky number, 9, and the advice of wizards and soothsayers. Here are some examples...

- He changed banknotes so they could be divided by the number 9 and declared that old banknotes were worthless. This caused most people in Burma to lose all of their savings.

- He was seen walking over a bridge backwards dressed as a king (apparently on the advice of his soothsayers).

- He believed bathing in dolphin's blood would keep him looking young.

- He ordered foreign companies to leave the country.

- He declared overnight that everyone should drive on the right-hand-side of the road instead of the left (again on the advice of his soothsayers).

BENJAMIN DISRAELI (1804–1881)

'The difference between a misfortune and a calamity is this: If Gladstone fell into the Thames, it would be a misfortune. But if someone dragged him out again, that would be a calamity.'

Benjamin Disraeli was a Conservative Prime Minister and William Gladstone was the leader of the opposition (the Liberals, then called the 'Whigs'). Throughout their careers, these two politicians simply detested each other!

MAD ABOUT...
DISNEY

When Disney released the film *Snow White and the Seven Dwarfs* in 1937 it won fans across the globe. Without doubt one of its most infamous fans was none other than Adolf Hitler.

The power-crazed dictator was known to own a copy of the film and he even enjoyed drawing the characters. After World War II ended, some of Hitler's doodles were found and they weren't that bad, either.

When he was younger, Hitler had hoped to be an artist, but nothing came of his dreams. If only he'd been more successful at painting, history would have been very different – who knows, he might even have got a job at Disney!

Did They Really Do That?

Sir Walter Raleigh (1552–1618)

'There are a nation of people whose heads appear not above their shoulders; which though it may be thought a mere fable, yet for mine own part I am resolved it is true, because every child in the provinces of Aromaia and Canuri affirm the same. They are called Ewaipanoma; they are reported to have their eyes in their shoulders, and their mouths in the middle of their breasts, and that a long train of hair groweth backward between their shoulders.'

So, Sir Walter, you didn't actually see these people when you travelled into South America, but you believe they exist because some children told you? Hmmmm. Perhaps they might have been pulling your leg...

Strike a light!

Blackbeard (1680–1718)

'Never play with matches'
goes the old saying – but
someone forgot to tell the
pirate Edward Teach, better
known as Blackbeard. Or perhaps
they didn't forget, maybe they just
thought they'd better not annoy him.

BARMY RATING: 3 OUT OF 5

Blackbeard was one of the maddest and baddest pirates of
the Caribbean – and there was plenty of competition. He
was so crazy he even shot one of his most trusted crew
members as a warning to the rest of the crew to remember
who was in charge!

Blackbeard was a pretty fearsome sight, too. He was a tall
man with wild black hair and a big bushy beard, and to make
himself look more fearsome he stuck long rope matches,
called tapers, under his hat – and then lit them.

Legend has it that when he died his headless corpse swam
around his ship three times – perhaps even the sharks were
too scared to eat him!

The empress who became the emperor

Wu Zetian (625–705)

Throughout the long history of Chinese emperors, there has been only one woman. There have been lots of empresses, but only one has been in charge and that's why Wu Zetian is called an emperor. She was a successful ruler, but to get from her humble beginnings to be in charge she had to be pretty sneaky.

Firstly she accused the empress of murder and of witchcraft. The emperor believed her lies, arrested his empress and married Wu Zetian. Later Wu would order that the old empress be murdered.

Then she had her oldest son exiled on charges of treason, and her middle son deposed when he became emperor following the death of Wu's husband. Her youngest son then became emperor, but she persuaded (forced) him to give up power so she could be in charge. Blimey!

CrackPot Quiz Question

Q. Lord Cardigan was in charge of the Light Brigade, a cavalry unit of the British Army during the Crimean War. When given an order to charge down a valley lined with enemy Russian cannons did he ...?

a) Realise it was a terrible idea and refuse;

b) Ask for confirmation of the order in case there was a mistake;

c) Go ahead and charge anyway.

And the answer is ... c) he went ahead and charged. It was a disaster. Of the 673 men who rode into the valley, around 200 were killed. Blame needs to be shared as it was by no means just Lord Cardigan's fault, but it appears he had no idea what a huge error he had made.

I'm sure it's China

Christopher Columbus (1451–1506)

Good old Columbus, discovering America and everything. The Americans even celebrate Columbus Day each year as a memorial to the great man. But was he actually that great? Hmm, it seems not.

Firstly, he never landed in North America. Although Columbus made four voyages he never set foot on mainland America. He actually visited some Caribbean islands (modern-day Haiti, the Dominican Republic and the Bahamas), Central America and South America.

Secondly, he didn't realise he had found a new country – or rather one new to Europeans (there were people living there already of course). Columbus was convinced he'd found a new way of getting to the Indies – that's Asia to you and me.

So how did he get it so wrong?

It seems that Columbus got the size of the world wrong. Despite the fact that the ancient Greeks had worked out the true size over a thousand years earlier, Columbus still managed to miscalculate – or he thought he knew better. Columbus actually thought the world was much smaller than it really is. So the Bahamas were roughly where he thought China should be.

So who did find North America first? No one knows for sure; it could have been the Viking, Leif Erikson, Irish monks, or even Basque fishermen. All we know for sure is that it definitely wasn't Columbus!

Welcome to China folks!

Fools!

MAD, BAD
and truly sticky
ENDINGS

Sigurd the Mighty (about 892 AD)

Sigurd the Mighty – or Sigurd Eysteinsson to give him his
real name – was one of the first earls of the island of Orkney.
Historians don't know a great deal about him apart from the
fact that he fought against a Scottish warlord called Máel Brigte
the Tusk (thanks to his prominent teeth).

The two warriors agreed to meet for a fight, bringing 40 men
each. Sigurd cheated and brought 80, and promptly massacred
his Scottish foes. He lopped off Máel Brigte's head for a trophy
and fastened it to his saddle. Unfortunately for Sigurd, as he
was riding home the head bashed against his leg and
Máel Brigte's teeth cut Sigurd's leg.
The wound became infected and
killed Sigurd.

Máel Brigte might have lost
his head but he still had the
last laugh!

MAD ABOUT...
SCOTLAND

Idi Amin of Uganda (c.1925–2003) was one of the most notorious African dictators ever and the cruelty of his reign was matched by some truly bizarre behaviour. He was rumoured to have sent love letters to the British queen, Elizabeth II, and also claimed to be the King of Scotland – even though he had no relatives from Scotland.

Perhaps strangest of all was the title he awarded himself, which was (I warn you, it's a bit of a mouthful):

His Excellency, President for Life, Field Marshal Al Hadji Doctor Idi Amin, VC, DSO, MC, CBE, Lord of all the Beasts of the Earth and Fishes of the Sea, and Conqueror of the British Empire in Africa in General and Uganda in Particular.

Imagine saying that every time your addressed him!

No boring fences here

Genghis Khan (1162–1227)

Think about ways you can mark out land that belongs to you. How about a nice fence, for example? Or a wall? Maybe even a sign, telling people who the land belongs to? Genghis Khan had a more arresting idea!

Genghis Khan was leader of the Mongol tribe of Central Asia. His warriors rampaged across Asia, sacking cities and striking fear everywhere they went. Much like Timur the Lame (see page 27), Genghis would mark his territory by building towers of skulls made from the heads of his defeated enemies. The idea was probably to warn and intimidate people.

Whatever the reason, Genghis had plenty of skulls to play with – some people claim he was responsible for the deaths of around 40 million people. His empire stretched all the way from Afghanistan in the west to northern China in the east – by far the biggest empire the world had ever seen. It wouldn't be matched until Britain started empire building in the 1800s.

Today Genghis is still considered a hero in his native Mongolia and in parts of China. In countries such as Afghanistan, they take a different point of view, regarding him to be some kind of devil. And if your relatives had been turned into part of a heap of heads, you probably would too!

MAD ABOUT...
GOLD

The Spanish conquistadors, who ventured into South and Central America to claim new lands and look for treasure, were a ruthless bunch. However, the worst of the lot was probably Lope de Aguirre.

He was so out of control that his fellow Conquistadors nicknamed him 'El Loco' (the madman). However, his behaviour really went off the rails during an expedition to find El Dorado – a mythical city of gold. Half-starved and frustrated at not finding the city, he killed the expedition leader, declared Peru independent of Spain (and even sent the Spanish king a rude letter telling him that), then killed a lot more people before being killed himself. And of course, he never found the mythical city.

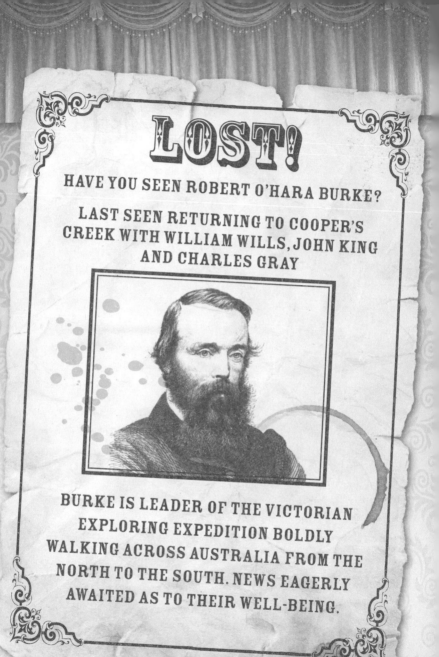

LOST!

HAVE YOU SEEN ROBERT O'HARA BURKE?

LAST SEEN RETURNING TO COOPER'S CREEK WITH WILLIAM WILLS, JOHN KING AND CHARLES GRAY

BURKE IS LEADER OF THE VICTORIAN EXPLORING EXPEDITION BOLDLY WALKING ACROSS AUSTRALIA FROM THE NORTH TO THE SOUTH. NEWS EAGERLY AWAITED AS TO THEIR WELL-BEING.

Desert drama

Robert O'Hara Burke (1820–1861)

They did eventually find Burke and the rest of his expedition, but by then only John King had survived. They had succeeded in their aim, but had perished doing so. Why?

Many people level much of the blame with Burke himself. He was totally unsuited to leading an expedition. He had no experience of exploring or of the Australian desert. He was wild, unpredictable and made rash decisions. Some people actually thought he was mad, thanks to the fact that he would take baths in his yard wearing a pith helmet.

He was also notorious for getting lost.

It's not much of a surprise it all went wrong. His expedition brought too much equipment, which slowed them down. Then when he decided to dump a lot of stuff, he left important things behind, like lime juice which would have kept them healthy. He also shunned the help of Aborigines – even scaring them off by firing his guns.

Tragically he, Wills and Gray starved to death. King survived after Aborigines saved him. Burke's mission had succeeded, but at a very high cost.

WILLIAM JOHN WILLS (1834–1861)

'These are probably the last lines you will ever get from me. We are on the point of starvation ... My spirits are excellent.'

William Wills was second-in-command to Robert O'Hara Burke on his ill-fated expedition to cross Australia on foot (see pages 72-73). Whereas Burke was a terrible explorer and highly impulsive, Wills was much more scientifically minded and as this quote proves, looked on the bright side of life.

Bother in the Bahamas

Juan Ponce de Leon (1460–1521)

Juan Ponce de Leon sailed with Christopher Columbus (see pages 66-67) on Columbus's second voyage to 'the Indies'. Unfortunately de Leon seems to have picked up Columbus's useless navigational skills on the way!

When Columbus returned to Spain, de Leon stayed on as Governor of Santo Domingo (what we now call the Dominican Republic). By all accounts he was a pretty ruthless ruler, so everyone must have been pleased when he decided to look for an island called Bimini. The island was said to have special water that gave you everlasting life.

He set off with three ships and he knew the island was in the Bahamas, but he just managed to miss it and find Florida instead. The bad news is that he thought it was a big island.

He set off to find Bimini again; and failed; again – and this time with more permanent results. When landing on Pine Island, his ship was attacked by the native people and de Leon was hit by a poisoned arrow. He died later of his wounds – if only he'd found that water!

The TEENAGE

Joan of Arc (1412–1431)

In the 1420s, life was tough for Charles VII of France. The English had invaded and were claiming France for themselves. Worse still, some of the French had sided with the English. Charles needed a brave warrior to lead them to victory!

But what he got was a 16-year-old farm girl who looked after the sheep and reckoned she spoke to angels.

The girl was Joan of Arc and, unlikely as it might have seemed, she was exactly what Charles needed. She told Charles that God was on his side – and despite being an uneducated peasant – turned out to be a brilliant military leader!

Her arrival must have come as a bit of a surprise to the French army – especially when she made them go to church and stop swearing. But Joan was probably an even bigger shock to the English forces. This brave shepherd girl, dressed in armour, charged into battle with the soldiers, carrying a banner and encouraging the French on to victory. And victorious they were, time and time again, and the English were forced to declare a truce.

It didn't end well for Joan though. She was captured and executed, but the girl with voices in her head had become a national hero and the English would ultimately be driven out of France.

Action Jackson

President Andrew Jackson (1767–1845)

You would imagine that the president of the USA would have to be cool, calm, rational and – importantly – not mad. Or angry. Or violent.

Someone didn't tell President Andrew Jackson.

For a start, he took part in duels with pistols against people he didn't like. He was known to have had at least 13 duels, but some historians think he may have had many, many more. In one duel – against a man who had insulted Jackson's wife – Jackson was shot but survived. The bullet stayed in his body for the rest of his life.

Jackson was an aggressive man. He once severely beat a man with his walking cane. Granted, the man had tried to assassinate him, but it's not the behaviour you expect of a president.

One story has it that Jackson's pet parrot came to his funeral. However, the bird had to be taken out because it kept saying swear words that it had heard Jackson using. Tut tut.

...@%$¢*!

Fu Manchu

Fu Manchu was a gang leader and master criminal who appeared in books, comics, radio and films from 1913 right through to the 1980s. His various dastardly plots involved kidnapping people, brainwashing, theft and murder and often included bizarre chemicals or venomous creatures.

Fu Manchu invented a formula for a drink – called his *elixir vitae* – that would let him live for an extended time, if not forever. This was very handy for writers as it meant they could keep writing Fu Manchu stories forever, too.

Fu Manchu was famous for his trademark moustache – a long, thin, droopy affair that reached down to his chest. It is now known as … a Fu Manchu!

The leader with two swords

Trieu Thi Trinh (c.222–248 AD)

Back in 43 AD, China invaded and took control of what we now call Vietnam. There were many rebellions against Chinese rule, but none were as famous as that led by Trieu Thi Trinh; this was remarkable for the times as she was a woman.

She raised an army and attacked the Chinese, winning at least 30 battles and scaring her enemies so much that they were said to be afraid to even look at her. She didn't hide during battles either – rather the reverse in fact. She rode on an elephant and wore golden armour, and was said to carry two swords.

She was eventually surrounded by the Chinese forces, but rather than surrender she flung herself into a river and drowned. She is still celebrated as being a great hero in Vietnam today.

King of the World

Homer Tomlinson (1892–1968)

What does a king or queen have that lets you know immediately that they are royalty? A crown perhaps, or maybe a palace or a golden carriage? Or how about a deckchair with 'King of all Nations' written on it by hand? A what?

That's what Homer Tomlinson had, and he claimed to be – well, as the chair says – King of all Nations.

Homer Tomlinson was a preacher in his own religion who ran for president of the USA in 1952. He didn't win (in case you didn't know) but that didn't stop him trying again in 1960 and in 1964 and finally in 1968. And then he gave up.

It didn't really matter though, because he was King of all Nations (he said) and travelled to 101 capital cities where he crowned himself to prove it. He had a crown, of course – he made it himself out of cardboard.

The President's

President Calvin Coolidge (1872–1933)

Calvin Coolidge, 30th President of the USA was famous for one thing in particular – being boring. He was President from 1923–1929 and he appeared to do nothing. He didn't speak much, and when the famous American wit Dorothy Parker heard he had died she remarked, 'How can they tell?'

However, Coolidge did have one surprising side to his character; he acquired a remarkable range of pets – enough for a small zoo. In no particular order he had:

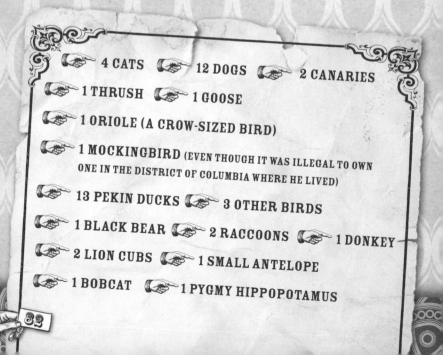

- 4 CATS
- 12 DOGS
- 2 CANARIES
- 1 THRUSH
- 1 GOOSE
- 1 ORIOLE (A CROW-SIZED BIRD)
- 1 MOCKINGBIRD (EVEN THOUGH IT WAS ILLEGAL TO OWN ONE IN THE DISTRICT OF COLUMBIA WHERE HE LIVED)
- 13 PEKIN DUCKS
- 3 OTHER BIRDS
- 1 BLACK BEAR
- 2 RACCOONS
- 1 DONKEY
- 2 LION CUBS
- 1 SMALL ANTELOPE
- 1 BOBCAT
- 1 PYGMY HIPPOPOTAMUS

mad menagerie

He didn't have all of them at the same time or try to keep all of them in the White House – that would be really mad – but a lot of them did live with him and his wife. The larger and more exotic animals were donated to a zoo where the President often went to visit them. He might have been boring, but he was crazy about animals!

MAD, BAD and truly sticky ENDINGS

Fools!

Francisco Pizarro (1478–1541)

Francisco Pizarro was a Spanish conquistador – an explorer who went to South America to plunder gold and riches. The conquistadors wiped out the Aztec and Inca empires and treated the native tribes of South America abysmally.

Pizarro was a particularly ruthless leader. He held the Incan emperor for ransom and then, when the ransom was paid, killed the emperor anyway. He dealt in a similarly brutal way with anyone who disagreed with him.

It seems quite fitting then that Pizarro was assassinated in Lima, the new city that he founded in Peru, by the family of one of his fellow explorers whom Pizarro had murdered.

Did They Really Do That?

CHRISTOPHER COLUMBUS (1451–1506)

'For the execution of the voyage to the Indies, I did not make use of intelligence, mathematics or maps.'

That would explain a lot, then (see pages 66-67).

QUEEN of the

Lady Hester Stanhope (1776–1839)

Lady Hester Stanhope lived the life of a true English eccentric. She left the social whirl of London behind and went exploring – venturing to places most Europeans feared to go!

The first thing that marks her out is her wardrobe. Lady Stanhope had to wear Middle Eastern-style men's clothes after losing hers in a shipwreck, and she found she liked them – they were comfortable, flamboyant and dramatic.

Lady S didn't travel light – she had 22 camels just to carry her belongings and arrived in places like a queen at the head of a royal procession. She must have looked very impressive, maybe it was this and her surprising personality that saw her avoid real danger.

The route she took from a place called Jaffa to Jerusalem (both in modern-day Israel) was riddled with bandits. Using her customary bravery and straight-forward nature, she rode directly to the most powerful of the bandit chiefs and demanded

DESERT

safe passage across – and she got it.

The undoubted high point of her life came when she visited the ruined city of Palmyra (in Syria). There the locals were so impressed with her that they crowned her 'Queen of the Desert' – and that was exactly how she wanted to be remembered.

MADE-UP MANIACS

Napoleon

Not Napoleon Bonaparte, who was a very real person, but Napoleon the pig from George Orwell's *Animal Farm* (1945). In the book, the animals of Manor Farm revolt against the farmer and take over the farm themselves.

The animals are meant to be equal, but Napoleon takes control. He gets rid of any animal that disagrees with him and forces the animals to work harder and harder, while he lives a life of luxury. By the end of the book, Napoleon has become a worse version of the original farmer.

The book is an allegory – a story where made-up characters represent real ones. In this case the farm represented Russia, and Napoleon was meant to be real-life dictator Joseph Stalin (see page 44).

MAD ABOUT...
PYRAMIDS

Egyptian pyramids were built as tombs for the kings of Egypt, the pharaohs. So, each pharaoh needed one pyramid; but not the pharaoh Sneferu (2613–2589 BC) – he had three built!

Pyramids take a great deal of time and effort to build, so what was Sneferu playing at? The truth was Sneferu was experimenting. He changed the design from old-fashioned step pyramids to the limestone-clad smooth-sided pyramids Egypt is famous for today. But it took a couple of goes to get it right.

The final pyramid – known as the Red Pyramid – was the tallest building in the entire world when it was completed. Although it is regarded as Sneferu's final resting place, his body has never been found – perhaps the pyramid wasn't finished in time!

The leopard that

Ashoka the Great (304–232 BC)

They say a leopard never changes its spots, meaning that people don't change the way they behave. Well the story of Ashoka the Great proves that's not necessarily true.

In the beginning, Ashoka was a warrior prince in what is now India, but when his father died he took control of his empire by murdering his brothers. He then decided to increase his empire by invading the neighbouring territories. He waged war after brutal war for around eight years. Eventually he controlled lands stretching from what is now Afghanistan to Bangladesh. He was one crazy fighting machine.

And then something odd happened.

Eat your greens!

changed its spots

Apparently Ashoka heard that one of his surviving brothers was hiding out in an area called Kalinga (present-day Orissa, India). Ashoka attacked and laid waste to the area, killing thousands of people. But when he saw what he had done he was horrified – all that death and destruction!

BARMY RATING: 2 OUT OF 5

So the leopard changed his spots. He embraced peace and non-violence and became a Buddhist, sending people across Asia and into Europe to spread the Buddhist message. He also became a vegetarian and forbade animals being killed and eaten in his empire. It wasn't just animals who benefited of course – he treated his subjects as equals and had wells dug and trees planted by roadsides to help weary travellers.

Many dictators are remembered through history for the evil they did, and Ashoka could have been one of them. Instead he is still revered for the *good* that he did – Ashoka the Great indeed!

THE BARMY

	519–465 BC	King Xerxes of Persia
	365–323 BC	Alexander the Great
👉	**300 BC**	**Rome starts invading other territories**
	304–232 BC	Ashoka the Great
	247–183 BC	Hannibal
	83–30 BC	Mark Antony
	406–453 AD	Attila the Hun
👉	**476 AD**	**End of the Roman Empire and start of the Byzantine Empire**
	625–705 AD	Wu Zetian
	950–1003	Erik the Red
👉	**1066**	**Norman Conquest of England**
	1118–1170	Thomas Becket
	1162–1227	Genghis Khan
	1318–1389	Pope Urban IV
👉	**1348–1350**	**The Black Death sweeps across Europe**
	1412–1431	Joan of Arc
	1431–1476	Vlad III
	1451–1506	Christopher Columbus
	1460–1521	Juan Ponce de Leon
	1478–1541	Francisco Pizarro
👉	**1492**	**Columbus 'discovers America'**
	1599–1652	Lord Byron

TIMELINE

1599–1658	Oliver Cromwell
1680–1718	Blackbeard
1702–1782	Anne Bonny
1728–1779	Captain James Cook
1755–1793	Marie Antoinette
1758–1794	Maximilien de Robespierre
1776–1839	Lady Hester Stanhope
☛ **1789–1799**	**French Revolution**
1707–1868	Lord Cardigan
1820–1861	Robert O'Hara Burke
1872–1933	President Calvin Coolidge
1878–1953	Joseph Stalin
1892–1968	Homer Tomlinson
1899–1947	Al Capone
1906–1996	Lieutenant Colonel 'Mad Jack' Churchill
1908–1985	Enver Hoxha
1911–2002	Ne Win
☛ **1914–1918**	**World War I**
1921–1996	Jean-Bédel Bokassa
1930–1997	Mobutu Sese Seko
☛ **1939–1945**	**World War II**

POLITE NOTICE: entries labelled with the
patented 'pointy finger' signify noteworthy
historical events – thank you.

93

Index

TOTALLY HOOKED?

UTTERLY GRIPPED?

Then turn over
to see our other
fabulously
bonkers titles...